Fraser Valley Regional Library

WONDERS OF CANADA

# SGang Gwaay

Annalise Bekkering

Weigl

CALGARY
www.weigl.com

Published by Weigl Educational Publishers Limited
6325 10th Street SE
Calgary, Alberta
T2H 2Z9

Website: www.weigl.com
Copyright ©2008 WEIGL EDUCATIONAL PUBLISHERS LIMITED
All rights reserved. No part of this publication may be reproduced, stored in a retrieval system, or transmitted in any form or by any means, electronic, mechanical, photocopying, recording, or otherwise, without the prior written permission of the publisher.

We acknowledge the financial support of the Government of Canada through the Book Publishing Industry Development Program (BPIDP) for our publishing activities.

Library and Archives Canada Cataloguing in Publication

Bekkering, Annalise
    SGang Gwaay / Annalise Bekkering.

(Wonders of Canada)
Includes index.
ISBN 978-1-55388-385-2 (bound)
ISBN 978-1-55388-386-9 (pbk.)

    1. Nan Sdins National Historic Site (B.C.)--Juvenile literature.  2. Haida Indians--History--Juvenile literature.  3. Haida Indians--Social life and customs--Juvenile literature.  4. World Heritage areas--British Columbia--Ninstints--Juvenile literature.  I. Title.  II. Series.
E99.H2B44 2007         j971.1'12            C2007-902255-3

Printed in the United States of America
1 2 3 4 5 6 7 8 9 0   11 10 09 08 07

**Project Coordinator**
Leia Tait

**Design**
Terry Paulhus

**Consultants**
Maggie Stronge and Barbara J. Wilson, Gwaii Haanas National Park Reserve and Haida Heritage Site

**Photograph and Text Credits**

Every reasonable effort has been made to trace ownership and to obtain permission to reprint copyright material. The publishers would be please to have any errors or omissions brought to their attention so that they may be corrected in subsequent printings.

**Courtesy of Gordon Miller**: page 8; **Library and Archives Canada**: page 11 left (PA-060009).

All of the Internet URLs given in the book were valid at the time of publication. However, due to the dynamic nature of the Internet, some addresses may have changed, or sites may have ceased to exist since publication. While the author and publisher regret any inconvenience this may cause readers, no responsibility for any such changes can be accepted by either the author or the publisher.

# Contents

Island of Memory .................... 4
Where in the World? ................. 6
A Trip Back in Time ................. 8
Becoming a World Heritage Site ...... 10
World Heritage in Canada ........... 12
Natural Wonders ................... 14
Cultural Treasures ................. 16
Amazing Attractions ................ 18
Issues in Heritage ................. 20
Build a Totem Pole ................. 22
Quiz/Further Research .............. 23
Glossary/Index ..................... 24

# Island of Memory

Imagine an island village frozen in time. Remains of longhouses stand on the mossy forest floor. Grey **mortuary** and **memorial** poles, once painted in bright colours, reach up toward the sky. Their carved faces look out over the ocean waves. An ancient forest darkens the horizon.

This is SGang Gwaay Llnagaay. It is a village on the island of SGang Gwaay near British Columbia. For 2,000 years, SGang Gwaay Llnagaay was home to the Kunghit Haida people. In the late 1800s, it was abandoned after most of its people died of disease. Today, SGang Gwaay Llnagaay is the world's best example of a **traditional** North West Coast **First Nations** village. The memorial and mortuary poles found here demonstrate the excellence achieved by the Haida in the 1800s. The poles provide a glimpse of Haida life before Europeans came to North America. They also demonstrate the Haida's close connection to nature. To protect the treasures found in SGang Gwaay Llnagaay, the entire island of SGang Gwaay was made a World Heritage site in 1981.

The poles at SGang Gwaay Llnaagay are very old. They have survived for hundreds of years.

# What is a World Heritage Site?

Heritage is what people inherit from those who lived before them. It is also what they pass down to future generations. Heritage is made up of many things. Objects, traditions, beliefs, values, places, and people are all part of heritage. Throughout history, these things have been **preserved**. A family's heritage is preserved in the stories, customs, and objects its members pass on to each other. Similarly, a common human heritage is preserved in the beliefs, objects, and places that have special meaning for all people, such as SGang Gwaay.

The United Nations Educational, Scientific and Cultural Organization (UNESCO) identifies places around the world that are important to all people. Some are important places in nature. Others are related to **culture**. These landmarks become World Heritage Sites. They are protected from being destroyed by **urbanization,** pollution, tourism, and neglect.

Carved faces decorate the totem poles in SGang Gwaay LInagaay.

You can learn more about UNESCO World Heritage Sites by visiting http://whc.unesco.org.

## Think about it

World Heritage Sites belong to all people. They provide a link to the past. These sites also help people from many cultures connect with each other. Think about your own heritage. What landmarks are important to you? Think about the places that have shaped your life. Make a list of your personal heritage sites. The list might include your home, your grandparents' home, your school, or any other place that is special to you and your family. Next to each location on the list, write down why it is important to you.

# Where in the World?

SGang Gwaay is a tiny island off the coast of British Columbia. It is part of the Queen Charlotte Islands. This is a group of islands in the Pacific Ocean, about 770 kilometres north of Vancouver. SGang Gwaay is the Haida name for the island. It means "Wailing Island," for the sound made by ocean waves rushing through a nearby reef. SGang Gwaay is also called Anthony Island. This is the name Europeans gave to the island when they came to the area.

SGang Gwaay Llnagaay is located on the eastern side of the island. The name is Haida for "Wailing Island Town." It is also sometimes called "Nan Sdins," after a former chief of the village. SGang Gwaay Llnagaay is built above a beach overlooking a small bay. The remains of 17 cedar longhouses are found here. The houses are nestled between more than 20 totem poles. Both the houses and the poles are made from cedar trees. They have stood here for hundreds of years, protected by the bay from ocean winds and rain.

■ Boaters can view SGang Gwaay Llnagaay from the water, but they cannot land at the village, as they might damage the fragile site. Instead, boaters must land on the north side of the island.

# Puzzler

The Queen Charlotte Islands are about 120 kilometres west of the city of Prince Rupert. They are separated from the mainland by a body of water called the Hecate Strait. Alaska lies to the north across a channel called the Dixon Entrance. To the south, a stretch of ocean called Queen Charlotte Sound divides the Queen Charlottes from Vancouver Island. SGang Gwaay lies off the southern tip of Moresby Island. This is the second-largest of the Queen Charlotte Islands. The largest is Graham Island, to the north. Using this information, match the names listed below to their locations on the map.

ANSWERS: 1. G  2. E  3. A  4. C  5. H  6. D  7. B  8. F

1. Alaska
2. Dixon Entrance
3. Prince Rupert
4. Hecate Strait
5. Moresby Island
6. Graham Island
7. Queen Charlotte Sound
8. Vancouver Island

# A Trip Back in Time

The Haida have lived on the Queen Charlotte Islands for more than 10,000 years. Their name for these islands is *Haida Gwaii*, or "island of the people." SGang Gwaay was once home to the Kunghit Haida. These were the most southerly of the Haida peoples. They were skilful hunters, fishers, and warriors, known for the richness of their culture and social structure.

SGang Gwaay Llnagaay began as a Kunghit hunting camp about 2,000 years ago. Over time, the camp grew into a village with many longhouses and totem poles carved from the island's giant cedar trees. Europeans first visited the island in the 1770s. They began trading with the Kunghit at SGang Gwaay Llnagaay. Soon, the area became an important centre for trade. However, Europeans brought disease to SGang Gwaay. In 1862, **smallpox** struck the Kunghit Haida. Most died. Those who survived moved away from the island. In SGang Gwaay Llnagaay, the population dropped from 300 to 30 in about 20 years. The last villagers left the island in 1884.

▬ At its peak, SGang Gwaay Llnagaay had about 20 longhouses and 300 people.

## Site Science

Carving the poles at SGang Gwaay Llnagaay was a great deal of work. All of the poles there were carved from cedar trees. Cedar wood is straighter, softer, and more durable than that of other trees. Carvers started by choosing a tall, thick tree. Once the tree was cut down, carvers removed the bark and smoothed the wood. They drew their design onto the cedar and carved it using tools made of wood, stone, bone, antler, and shell.

The figures on mortuary and memorial poles were designed to tell a story. The most important figures in the story were at the bottom of the pole. Carvers worked on these images first. The figures were detailed, since observers would see them up close.

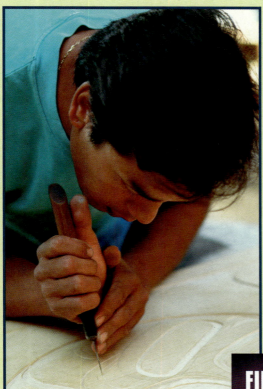

Large poles took many months to finish carving. When carving was done, the poles were painted. Paints were made from natural substances such as animal oils, charcoal, ochre, and moss. When a pole was finished, the Haida held a special ceremony to celebrate and raise the pole in its chosen location.

▬ Today, Haida artists use both traditional and modern tools to create memorial and mortuary poles.

**FIND MORE ONLINE**

See examples of Haida totem poles at www.k12.nf.ca/stbernards/totem.

# Becoming a World Heritage Site

After the last villagers left SGang Gwaay, the island lay empty for many years. Few people outside of the Haida community knew it existed.

In the 1930s, the British Columbia government became interested in SGang Gwaay. In 1957, it moved 15 of the island's totem poles to museums in Vancouver and Victoria. The government created Anthony Island Provincial Park in 1958 to protect the remaining poles and longhouse remains at SGang Gwaay Llnagaay. In 1981, the Canadian government asked UNESCO to make SGang Gwaay a World Heritage site. UNESCO agreed. SGang Gwaay became a UNESCO World Heritage Site on October 30, 1981.

▬ Twenty memorial and mortuary poles remain at SGang Gwaay today. They are the world's largest collection of such poles still in their original location.

## Heritage Heroes

Tom Price was the last chief of SGang Gwaay Llnagaay. He was born in the village in 1860. As a young man, Tom Price **inherited** the title of head chief of SGang Gwaay Llnagaay. By then, the village was almost empty. Soon, Tom Price and his family decided to leave SGang Gwaay. Around 1875, they moved to Skidegate, a larger Haida village on a nearby island. That is where the Kunghit Haida went after leaving SGang Gwaay.

At Skidegate, Tom Price was recognized as a leader for the Kunghit people. He helped gather and record the traditions of SGang Gwaay. He also helped preserve knowledge of the island. Tom Price provided scholars with Kunghit place names and village locations. He shared the legends that explained his people's beliefs and told their history. At Skidegate, Tom Price learned to carve objects made of silver and wood. He used this new skill to carve the legends and symbols of the Kunghit people into pipes, bowls, and small totem poles. In this way, Tom Price helped ensure that the culture and heritage of SGang Gwaay was not lost.

▬ After Tom died in 1927, no one else inherited the title of chief.

# Wonders of Canada

# World Heritage in CANADA

There are more than 800 UNESCO World Heritage Sites in 138 countries around the globe. Canada has 14 of these sites. Seven are natural sites, and seven are cultural sites. Each is believed to be of outstanding heritage value to all people around the world. Look at the map. Are any of these sites near your home? Have you visited any of them? Learn more about World Heritage Sites in Canada by visiting www.pc.gc.ca/progs/spm-whs/itm2-/index_e.asp.

### Canadian Rocky Mountain Parks (Alberta and British Columbia)
- A mountain landscape created by North America's largest mountain range

### The Historic District of Old-Quebec (Quebec)
- The only walled city north of Mexico
- The the birthplace of French culture in North America

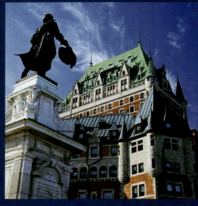

### Wood Buffalo National Park (Alberta and Northwest Territories)
- The site of the largest inland freshwater delta in the world

**LEGEND**
- 🟡 = Natural Landmarks
- 🔴 = Cultural Sites

**SCALE** 0 — 269 Kilometres

1. Canadian Rocky Mountain Parks (Alberta and British Columbia)
2. Dinosaur Provincial Park (Alberta)
3. Gros Morne National Park (Newfoundland and Labrador)
4. Head-Smashed-In Buffalo Jump (Alberta)

SGang Gwaay 13

- 5 The Historic District of Old-Quebec (Quebec)
- 6 Kluane/Wrangell-St Elias/Glacier Bay/Tatshenshini-Alsek (British Columbia, Yukon, and Alaska)
- 7 L'Anse aux Meadows National Historic Site (Newfoundland and Labrador)
- 8 Miguasha National Park (Quebec)
- 9 Nahanni National Park Reserve (Northwest Territories)
- 10 Old Town Lunenburg (Nova Scotia)
- 11 Rideau Canal (Ontario)
- 12 SGang Gwaay (British Columbia)
- 13 Waterton Glacier International Peace Park (Alberta and Montana)
- 14 Wood Buffalo National Park (Alberta and Northwest Territories)

# Natural Wonders

Separated from the British Columbia mainland by the Hecate Strait, SGang Gwaay and the other islands of Haida Gwaii are home to many unique plants and animals. Some, including 15 **species** of stickleback fish, cannot be found any other place on Earth. Others, such as the Queen Charlotte black bear, are very different from their relatives on the mainland.

The southern islands of Haida Gwaii, including SGang Gwaay, form the Gwaii Haanas National Park **Reserve**. Here, coastal rain forests of giant Sitka spruce and cedar are home to animals such as the pine marten and the dusky shrew. Huge colonies of bald eagles and Peregrine falcons nest along the coastline. They are joined by about 750,000 seabirds, including ancient murrelets, tufted and horned puffins, and auklets. Offshore, the waters are filled with sea lions, dolphins, porpoises, and harbour seals. Fish, shellfish, sea urchin, and octopus are plentiful. Many whales, including orcas and humpbacks, can often be seen gliding through the waters.

The waters off SGang Gwaay are a key mating spot for large numbers of Steller sea lions.

**FIND MORE ONLINE**

Plan a visit to Gwaii Haanas National Park Reserve and Haida Heritage Site at www.pc.gc.ca/pn-np/bc/gwaii haanas/index_e.asp.

## Creature Feature

The Haida have shared the land with bears for thousands of years. They have great respect for these animals. Bears are symbols of power and strength in Haida stories and art. They are treated as friends. The Haida name for bear is *Taan*, or "brother of man."

The Queen Charlotte black bear is only found on Haida Gwaii. Queen Charlotte black bears have lived on these islands for at least 10,000 years. They look different from other black bears, which can have black, cinnamon, brown, or blonde fur. Queen Charlotte black bears only have black fur.

All black bears are omnivores. This means they eat both meat and plants. On Haida Gwaii, salmon is the main source of food for black bears. They also eat crabs, clams, and other hard-shelled sea creatures found along the shoreline. As a result, Queen Charlotte black bears have remarkably strong jaws. They also have larger heads and larger molar teeth than other black bears.

■ Queen Charlotte black bears are the largest black bears in the world.

# Cultural Treasures

When the Kunghit people left SGang Gwaay in the 1800s, they joined other Haida groups in villages such as Skidegate and Old Masset. Their customs and traditions became blended with these groups. Over time, the Haida population grew again. There are now more than 4,000 Haida living mainly in British Columbia and Alaska. Many still live on Haida Gwaii and continue to hunt and fish as part of their lifestyle.

Today, Haida culture is thriving. The Haida have become known around the world for their art and craftsmanship. Haida artists, such as the late Bill Reid, learned traditional styles and methods from Haida elders known as Old Masters. Today, Haida artists trained by the Old Masters create traditional Haida poles, masks, blankets, clothing, and embroidered goods that are sold around the world. These artists carry on the artistic traditions that have shaped Haida culture for thousands of years.

▬ The main style of Haida art is called flat design. Black outlines are used to create forms that are filled in with red colour. Flat design is used to decorate totem poles and other items, such as masks and traditional clothing worn by Haida dancers.

## Telling Tales

**Haida art often features images taken from traditional stories. Like all cultures, the Haida use stories to explain how the world works. This Haida tale describes how Raven discovered the first Haida people.**

Raven looked up the beach and saw that he was all alone. There was no one for him to play tricks on. Raven let out a sad cry. Suddenly, he heard a small squeak and saw something white in the sand.

Buried in the sand was a giant clamshell. The squeaking noise was coming from inside the clamshell. Raven looked inside and saw some tiny creatures. The creatures were afraid of him. They would not come out of the clamshell. Raven wanted them to come out so he could play with them.

Raven was a sly trickster. He used a lovely song to charm the creatures out of the clamshell. The creatures were curious about the song. They came out of the clamshell.

The creatures were very different from Raven. They did not have any feathers, fur, or a beak. These creatures were the first Haida people. Raven wanted to protect the people so he would not be alone anymore. He provided them with fire, salmon, and cedar to help them live.

# Amazing Attractions

There is much to explore on a visit to SGang Gwaay. Visitors travel by boat to the island's north beach. From there, they hike through the forest to SGang Gwaay Llnagaay. Through the dense, old trees, visitors can explore the poles and longhouse remains for a glimpse of Haida life in the past.

In front of what was once the chief's house, there are three tall totem poles. Each pole is topped by a male figure wearing a tall hat. These figures are called the "watchmen." One watchman faces the ocean. The other two look over the village. The Haida believed these watchmen had **supernatural** powers and would protect the village by warning the chief of coming danger.

Today, people act as "watchmen." Between May and September each year, four Haida Gwaii watchmen live on the island. They protect the site from damage by people and nature, and provide visitors with information. The watchmen are the only people who live on SGang Gwaay.

SGang Gwaay watchmen share Haida culture with visitors through traditional stories, songs, and dances.

SGang Gwaay   19

## Featured Attraction

Most of the totem poles at SGang Gwaay Llnagaay are mortuary poles. Mortuary poles have a box at the top called a grave box. The grave box was used to hold the remains of important people from the village, such as chiefs. Below the box, the poles were carved with symbols of the person who died. These included both natural and supernatural images.

All of the mortuary poles at SGang Gwaay Llnagaay are more than 100 years old. Many of their carvings have worn away over time. Some can still be seen, but their meanings are no longer known. Even so, they are the best collection of Haida mortuary poles in the world.

**KEY ISSUES**

# Issues in Heritage

Protecting SGang Gwaay can be difficult. Hundreds of years of sunlight, wind, and rain have bleached and **eroded** the wooden remains. Plants have pushed their way between cracks in the cedar. Animals have damaged the totem poles by rubbing against them and nesting inside. Before the island was protected as a heritage site, treasure hunters stole many **artifacts**. Today, about 1,600 tourists visit the island each year. Sometimes, they harm the totem poles and longhouse remains by touching them or walking on them.

The Canadian government and the Council of the Haida Nation have taken special steps to help solve these issues. They have limited visitor groups to 12 people at a time. Twice each year, trees, bushes and other plants growing too near the totem poles are removed. In 1995 and 1997, some leaning poles were straightened to keep them standing as long as possible. Some people have suggested removing all of the remaining poles for permanent protection, but this is not the wish of the Haida.

Experts often examine the poles to learn more about the site's history.

**FIND MORE ONLINE**

Help protect World Heritage Sites like SGang Gwaay at http://whc.unesco.org/education.

# Should the remaining totem poles on SGang Gwaay be moved to museums?

| YES | NO |
|---|---|
| The totem poles would last much longer if they were preserved in museums, since they would be protected from the Sun, wind, rain, animals, and people. | The Haida believe the cedar poles should be allowed to return to the earth, where they came from. The poles were not intended to last forever.  |
| More people would be able to see the poles in museums on the mainland.  | People can already see 15 poles that were taken from SGang Gwaay in the mid-1900s to be shown in museums. |
| The Canadian government and the Haida peoples would not have to spend as much time and money to preserve the site. |  SGang Gwaay displays totem poles in the natural environment, as they were meant to be seen. The poles show the connection the Haida peoples have with nature. |

**Think about this issue. Are there any possible solutions that would satisfy both sides of the debate?**

# Build a Totem Pole

**Materials Needed**
A large bowl, four or five plastic bottles or soda cans of different sizes and shapes, newspaper, flour, sand, measuring cup, water, white paint, coloured paints, paintbrushes, cardboard, strong tape

**1** Choose a bottle or can for the bottom of your totem pole. Fill it with sand, and secure the top with a lid. This will make it heavy and stop the pole from tipping easily.

**2** Tape the cans and bottles together end-to-end in the order you think is most interesting.

**3** Use cardboard to make features that will stick out from your totem pole, such as wings or beaks. Cut out the shapes with your scissors. Use tape to attach the shapes to your pole.

**4** In a bowl, mix 250 millilitres of flour with 500 millilitres of water to create a paste. Stir the mixture well to remove all the lumps.

**5** Tear strips of newspaper about 3 centimetres wide. Dip the strips in the paste until they are coated. Then, smooth them onto your totem pole to create a surface you can paint. Completely cover the pole with coated strips. Let it dry for a few hours.

**6** When the pole is dry, paint it white. Wait for the paint to dry.

**7** Use coloured paint to decorate the totem pole with different symbols. These can be animals or any other symbols you choose.

**8** When the totem pole is finished, write a story about the characters on the pole. Remember that the character at the bottom of the pole should be the most important.

# Quiz

1. What type of wood are the totem poles on SGang Gwaay made out of?
2. In what year did SGang Gwaay become a World Heritage Site?
3. What illness forced the Kunghit Haida to leave SGang Gwaay?
4. Who was the last chief of SGang Gwaay?
5. How many people visit SGang Gwaay every year?

**ANSWERS:** 1. cedar  2. 1981  3. smallpox  4. Tom Price  5. about 1,600

# Further Research

You can find more information on SGang Gwaay at your local library or on the Internet.

### Libraries
Most libraries have computers that connect to a database for researching information. If you input a key word, you will be provided with a list of books in the library that contain information on that topic. Non-fiction books are arranged numerically, using their call number. Fiction books are organized alphabetically by the author's last name.

### Websites
Learn about other communities on Haida Gwaii by visiting
**www.civilization.ca/aborig/haida/havhg01e.html**.

Experience the Haida way of life at
**www.virtualmuseum.ca/Exhibitions/Haida**.

# Glossary

**artifacts:** objects used or made by humans long ago

**culture:** the characteristics, beliefs, and practices of a racial, religious, or social group

**eroded:** worn away by water, wind, or ice

**First Nations:** members of Canada's Aboriginal community who are not Inuit or Métis; the first peoples to live in what is now Canada

**inherited:** legally received something from a person after his or her death

**memorial:** serving to preserve the memory of a person or an event

**mortuary:** relating to death or the burial of the dead

**preserved:** protected from injury, loss, or ruin

**reserve:** land set aside by the Canadian government to protect plants and wildlife

**smallpox:** a disease that causes a fever and a skin rash, which was often deadly in the past

**species:** groups of plants or animals that share the same characteristics

**supernatural:** relating to things that exist outside the laws of nature and the visible world, such as gods and spirits

**traditional:** having to do with established beliefs or practices

**urbanization:** the movement of people out of the countryside and into cities

# Index

animals  14, 15, 20, 21, 22
art  4, 15, 16, 17

British Columbia  4, 6, 10, 12, 13, 16

cedar  6, 8, 9, 14, 17, 20, 21, 23

Gwaii Hanaas  14, 15

Haida  4, 6, 8, 9, 10, 11, 15, 16, 17, 18, 19, 20, 21, 23
history  4, 5, 8, 10, 11

issues  20, 21

longhouses  6, 8, 10, 18, 20

mortuary and memorial poles  4, 5, 6, 8, 9, 10, 11, 16, 18, 19, 20, 21, 22, 23

plants  14, 15, 20
Price, Tom  11, 23

Queen Charlotte Islands (Haida Gwaii)  6, 7, 8, 14, 15, 16, 18, 23

Reid, Bill  16

SGang Gwaay Llnagaay  4, 5, 6, 8, 10, 11, 16, 18, 19
smallpox  8, 23
stories  17, 18

United Nations Educational, Scientific and Cultural Organization (UNESCO)  5, 10, 12

watchmen  18
World Heritage Sites  4, 5, 10, 12, 13, 20, 23